Original title:
The Ocean's Lullaby

Copyright © 2025 Creative Arts Management OÜ
All rights reserved.

Author: Nolan Kingsley
ISBN HARDBACK: 978-1-80587-435-5
ISBN PAPERBACK: 978-1-80587-905-3

### **Crashing Waves of Calm**

Waves make faces, splash and smile,
Seagulls laugh and glide in style.
Fish hold contests, who can flip?
A crab takes bets on its next trip.

Surfboards dance with a twist and shout,
A dolphin grins as it swims about.
Hermit crabs wear shells so bright,
Chasing shadows until the night.

## Breezes that Soothe

Gentle breezes tickle my nose,
Whispers of tangy seaweed grows.
Sandcastles cringe at the tide's tease,
As crabs dart quick with such expert ease.

Kites tangled in seaweed play,
While clams gossip the day away.
In this windy show, we sway,
Laughing while the ocean holds sway.

## Resting in the Nereid's Arms

Mermaids giggle, brushing their hair,
Shells act as microphones, Oh, what flair!
Seashells compete for the best voice,
A dolphin's flip prompts a dance choice.

Underwater music plays so sweet,
Anemones sway to a soft beat.
We rest in laughter, the waves our song,
Where silly fish join and all belong.

**Twilight's Embrace on the Seashore**

Twilight brings a canvas bold,
As waves release secrets untold.
To starfish spinning, we clap and cheer,
As laughter rings out—nothing to fear!

Crashing tides hum a merry tune,
Jellyfish twirl 'neath the glowing moon.
With sand beneath, we sigh and beam,
Beneath starlight, we weave our dream.

**Quietude of the Sea Breeze**

A seagull snores upon the shore,
While crabs dance tango on the floor.
The sunbeams tickle silly toes,
As fish wear hats made out of bows.

The sand smiles back, it's quite a sight,
As starfish giggle in pure delight.
The breeze sings tunes of silly cheer,
While turtles flirt with passing deer.

## **Bubbles of Sweet Dreams**


Bubbles pop like tiny balloons,
While dolphins hum enchanting tunes.
A whale's big grin is hard to beat,
As fish play tag with swaying seaweed.

Mermaids braid their hair with kelp,
And crabs recite their jokes with yelp.
In this world where laughter flows,
Even sea cucumbers strike a pose.

## **Flotsam Fantasies**

Old flip-flops float in grand parade,
While jellybeans in currents wade.
A rubber duck sails with great flair,
As sea urchins trade style tips with care.

Seaweed wiggles like a dance floor,
And seashells chatter, wanting more.
With laughter echoing through the spray,
Every wave shouts, hip-hip-hooray!

**Waves of Repose**

The tide rolls in, a playful tease,
As crabs play poker 'neath the trees.
Fish wear glasses, all so chic,
They gossip softly, oh what a sneak!

A sea cucumber slips on a hat,
While plankton giggle, imagine that!
With each wave's lilt, the silliness grows,
Making waves is how the fun flows.

**Lagoon's Lull**

In the lagoon, fish like to prance,
Wiggling their tails in a water dance.
Crabs wear hats made of seaweed green,
Chasing each other like it's a scene.

Turtles slow dance with jellyfish friends,
Offering tips on how to make amends.
Starfish flip-flop in their shiny suits,
Collecting gossip from giggling brutes.

## Seabreeze Silhouettes


Seagulls gossip with sandy seashells,
Trading secrets and oceanic spells.
The waves sneak up to tickle our toes,
Saying, "Frolic while the breeze softly blows!"

Fish don tuxedos to join the parade,
Dancing with stars in an ocean charade.
Whales wear sunglasses, they strut with flair,
While dolphins do flips with the utmost care.

**Calm Before the Ocean's Awakening**

Before the tide turns, seahorses nap,
Building blanket forts in a kelp-wrap.
Crabs don pajamas, snoring away,
As clams dream of dances they'll brava today.

Seals play charades with the shy seaweed,
Mimicking poses, a hilarious creed.
With a wink from a fish, the night starts to gleam,
And laughter erupts like a frothy dream.

## Murmurs Under Moonlight

Under the moon, the ocean hums light,
Starfish giggle as the waves say, "Goodnight!"
Turtlenecks make jokes, oh what a sight,
While crabs throw a party, their eyes shining bright.

With shells as their hats, they dance in delight,
Creating a ruckus, a truly fun plight.
Dolphins dive deep, then leap in the air,
While the sea whispers secrets, quirky and rare.

## Whispers of the Tides

The crab did jig on sandy floor,
While seagulls squawked and tried to soar.
A clam declared it was no crime,
To dance like this at lunch time!

Fish in schools were up to tricks,
Playing tag, dodging quick fix.
The octopus waved with a grin,
Saying, "Join us, come on in!"

## **Melodies Beneath the Waves**

A jellyfish floated like a balloon,
Dropping beats to a funky tune.
While sea turtles, wise and grand,
Took up salsa on the sand!

Eels did twist and sway with flair,
Bubbles rising without a care.
Even the crabs clapped their claws,
Joining in with laughter's paws!

## Serenade of the Seabreeze

Two shrimp sang duets, quite off-key,
Annoying fish, but carefree.
A whale in the back tried to hum,
While dolphins jumped—what a fun!

Sea urchins grinned, their spines in cheer,
As sand dollars spun, full of beer.
The seahorses twirled in glee,
Wishing for a new TV!

**Dreaming with the Dolphins**

With flips and flops, they stole the show,
Dolphins danced while others rowed.
Their laughter echoed, a watery beat,
As they leapt and spun, oh so fleet!

Clownfish chuckled, sharing jokes,
While sly sea otters played with floats.
In this ball of fun, all played along,
As the tides sang sweet, silly songs!

## Murmurs at Midnight

The waves whisper tales of sleepy fish,
Who wear tiny pajamas, dreaming of a dish.
Seagulls snore softly, their beaks in the sand,
While crabs do the cha-cha, a dance so unplanned.

Stars twinkle and giggle, they know all the jokes,
"Why did the clam blush?" they tease with their pokes.
The tide rolls in laughter, tickling the shore,
As shells gossip loudly, always wanting more.

## Ocean's Embrace of Slumber

A turtle in flip-flops takes a stroll at night,
While starfish play cards, giggling at their plight.
The moon winks wisely at each silly sight,
As dolphins wear pajamas, dancing with delight.

"Hey squid, do a cannonball!" calls out a friend,
With splashes and laughter that never will end.
Seashells sing sweetly, their voices in tune,
As jellyfish float by, and dance with the moon.

## Floating on Celestial Waters

Fish in fluffy beds of seaweed do nap,
While octopuses juggle, perhaps a bit rap.
A shrimp with a tiara leads a conga line,
As the water sways gently, oh, isn't it fine?

Crabs ride on the back of a whale full of dreams,
Sailing through starry skies, or so it seems.
The bubbles start bubbling with giggles galore,
As tides tickle stars on the sandy sea floor.

## Sandy Sighs in Twilight

At dusk, the beach bunnies gather to chat,
In hats made of shells, how silly is that?
They gossip 'bout crabs and their failed attempts,
At starting a band with their hyper pretense.

A clam with a mustache claims he's quite a star,
While the seaweed dances, and sways from afar.
Stars start to sparkle, painting waves bright,
And everyone chuckles, "Good night, and good night!"

## Beneath the Brine's Gentle Caress

Waves giggle as they lap the shore,
Starfish crack jokes, they're never a bore.
Seagulls mimic laughter, a chorus at play,
Turtles dance gently, in water ballet.

Jellyfish juggle, a sight to behold,
Crabs throw a party, their stories retold.
Seaweed sways softly, like hair in the breeze,
Clownfish are bright, always aiming to tease.

## Nautical Nurturing

Bubbles tickle fish, with a bubbly embrace,
Seashells share wisdom, at a leisurely pace.
A dolphin plays fetch, with a starry-eyed whale,
Together they spiral, leaving a sparkling trail.

Octopi offer hugs, with arms all around,
They launch into laughter, echoing the sound.
Children of the tide, joyful and spry,
Chasing each other, beneath the sea sky.

## Silence Beneath the Surface

Subtle whispers flow, beneath the cool blue,
Fish giggle and wiggle, with a hop and a boo.
Coral reef parties, full of color and zest,
Every little creature, doing its best.

Silent sea cucumbers, plotting a show,
They'll tell the best tales, you'll want to know.
Seahorses twirl round, in a waltz so divine,
The depth is alive, and wonderfully fine.

**Currents of Comfort**

Gentle swells cradle, in a cozy embrace,
Starfish on lounge chairs, taking up space.
Worms wear their shades, in the sandy delight,
While squids spin in circles, just for the light.

Barnacles gossip, glued on their throne,
Claiming the driftwood, that's all their own.
Mollusks hum tunes, with shells all aglow,
In this funny world, where the currents flow.

## **Dreaming Beyond the Horizon**

As fish wear tiny hats and grin,
They swim about, let giggles begin.
Seagulls sing in playful jest,
Bringing laughter on a crest.

But watch the crab with tipsy dance,
He trips on sand, a clumsy prance.
Starfish giggle as they play,
Waving their arms, they steal the day.

**Cradle of the Sea**

A turtle snores, as waves embrace,
His shell a pillow in this soft space.
Octopus serves drinks with a flair,
Tentacles mixing in salty air.

But clams complain, they're out of style,
Their shells are dull, they need a smile.
The plankton laugh, a tiny crowd,
Dancing together, they're quite proud.

## Moonlit Waters

The moonlight winks on the rippling tides,
Fish in pajamas, oh how they glide.
Lobster in shades, under a star,
Claims he's the coolest by far.

But jellyfish float, dressed in glow,
Swaying softly, putting on a show.
The crab keeps checking his clock,
Just to be late, it's part of his schlock.

## Symphony of Salt and Sand

The waves play music, a silly tune,
Sandcastles dance under the moon.
Seashells gossip about the tide,
Whispering tales of day and pride.

But dolphins juggle while swimming by,
With beach balls and laughter in the sky.
Crabs tap dance with shells on their feet,
In a salty rhythm, they can't be beat.

## Slumbering Shores

Waves giggle as they crash on sand,
Seagulls squawk, a funny band.
Crabs dance sideways in the sun,
Whispers of the sea, endless fun.

Shells are hats for starfish play,
While jellyfish float in disarray.
Sandcastles fall from a playful breeze,
Shellfish chuckle with such ease.

Beach balls bounce with a gentle plop,
As sunbathers snooze and flip-flop.
The tide retreats with a sleepy sigh,
As sea cucumbers wink goodbye.

Sand in shorts, a common plight,
Yet laughter lingers in their sight.
With every wave, a chuckle's born,
At slumbering shores, all woes are worn.

**Echoes Beneath the Waves**

Bubbles pop with giggling flair,
Fish swim by with nary a care.
The seaweed sways like a silly dance,
Caught in a tide of playful chance.

Octopuses wear a grand disguise,
As they juggle bubbles with their eyes.
Mermaids slurp from a coconut shell,
Sharing secrets only fish can tell.

The clam jokes with its shell so tight,
"Why did the fish sleep all night?"
"Because the current whisked it away,
To dream of shrimp in a ballet!"

Echoes laugh beneath the blue,
Where dolphins dive and join the crew.
Beneath the waves, all pranks unfold,
In a realm where mischief's gold.

## Seraphic Coastline

At dawn, the shore greets yawning shells,
Sandy pixies ring their bells.
Seasalt tickles the noses of dreams,
While the coastline giggles with sunny beams.

Seashells trade truths with crafty gulls,
As laughter echoes, sweet and full.
The sunbeams dance with the driftwood's sway,
Making beachcombers laugh and play.

Barnacles sport tiny hats of foam,
As they settle down, far from home.
The tides turn tales with a wink and grin,
As crabs tell secrets they keep within.

Seraphic shores, where fun's the theme,
Bring bubbles to life and wishful dreams.
With every splash, joy ignites,
In this coastline of giggles and delights.

## A Soft Salutation from the Sea

Waves tickle toes like a playful friend,
Seagulls squawk, their antics never end.
Mermaids giggle with shells in their hair,
Fish play hide and seek without a care.

The tide does a dance in a wobbly way,
While crabs in top hats join in the fray.
Jellyfish float like balloons gone astray,
The seaweed winks, saying, 'Come out and play!'

## **Harmony in the Foamy Embrace**

Foamy hugs wrapping round a sandy shore,
Turtles tiptoe, then start to explore.
Starfish in shades sipping sun by the tide,
Lobsters in bow ties, they cannot hide.

With a splash and a dash, the dolphins leap,
Belly-flops happen, with laughter to keep.
Octopuses juggle, each one a delight,
As beach balls bounce in quite silly flight.

## **Undercurrents of Peace**

Bubbles giggle when they rise to the top,
Clams hold tea parties, never a flop.
A whale sings operas, so big and so grand,
While crabs line dance on a golden sand.

The current mischievously swirls all about,
Tickling fish who can't help but shout.
Seashells gossip as waves roll in fast,
With laughter and joy, making moments last.

## **Coastline Serenade**

Sandcastle kingdoms where dreams come alive,
Shovels and buckets, oh, how they thrive!
Puddles reflecting the sun's golden rays,
As gulls set the stage for their showbiz plays.

A beach ball giggles as it rolls away,
While flip-flops argue about who will stay.
Seashells are judges, getting quite involved,
In this playful ruckus of sunny resolve.

### Echoes of the Deep Blue

Fish wear pajamas, snug and tight,
Seaweed dances in the soft moonlight.
Crabs have crumpets, oh what a sight,
Waves chuckle softly, all through the night.

Octopus juggles with shells galore,
Seahorses play hopscotch on the ocean floor.
Jellyfish bounce, they can't help but snore,
The deep blue giggles, who could ask for more?

**Nautical Naps**

Dolphins dreaming of silly tricks,
Mermaids gossip with starfish flicks.
Turtles snore, while the waves tick-tick,
As whales hum tunes, that just make you gig.

Clams in pajamas, all cozied and tight,
Crabs sip tea, ready for night.
Seagulls yawn loudly, holding on tight,
To dreams of fish fries, what a delight!

**Salty Sighs at Dusk**

Seashells whisper the silliest tales,
Of fish in tuxedos with tiny scales.
Starfish chuckle while riding the gales,
As sand crabs dance with their wobbly flails.

The sunset giggles, painting the sea,
Forgetful otters lose all their keys.
A clam-shark wears glasses, so cheesy,
What a soirée, oh come join with glee!

## Driftwood Dreams

Logs in pajamas, driftwood on the bay,
Snoring beach balls, what do they say?
The sand makes a blanket, oh so gray,
As surfboards gather for a cheeky play.

Flip-flops argue about sandals' flair,
Seashells sing tunes with salt in the air.
The tide rolls in, with the softest care,
In this wacky world, nothing's unfair!

## Whispers of the Seafoam

The waves sneak in, a giggling tide,
They tickle toes while we try to hide.
Sea gulls squawk, think they're the boss,
But we know they just want our lunch toss.

A starfish winks, it's quite a sight,
It did a dance under the moonlight.
The crab tries to pinch, but we run away,
Laughing out loud, it's a silly play.

**Dreams Adrift on Salty Air**

A dolphin flips, in the sun's bright glow,
It spins and twirls, putting on a show.
Fish toss a party, don't be late,
They're socking it to us with salmon strait.

Tides giggle as they roll on the sand,
Shells wear funny hats, oh isn't it grand?
Mermaids sing tipsy, in seashell bars,
While we all dance, under the stars.

## Comfort in the Coastal Breeze

The breeze whispers tales of mischief and glee,
It tousles our hair, just wait and see.
A sandcastle stands, but it wobbles a bit,
Watch out! Here comes a wave, with a cheeky hit!

The crabs conspire in their sandy lair,
Planning a sneak attack with flails in the air.
We burst out laughing, with sand in our toes,
As the ocean just giggles, that's how it goes.

## Submerged Serenades

Under the sea, where the funny fish gleam,
They wiggle and jiggle in a watery dream.
An octopus juggles with shells on its head,
   While a turtle snoozes in a coral bed.

The bubbles rise high, like balloons in flight,
   Blowing kisses to the stars at night.
   All the sea creatures join in the fun,
For a raucous concert, until the day is done.

## Currents of Comfort

Waves dance and splash, what a sight,
Seagulls squawking with delight.
Flip-flops flying, kids in a race,
Each tumble brings a salty embrace.

Sandcastles topple, they just can't stand,
A bucket's broken, oh, isn't it grand?
Crabs pinch toes with a sly little grin,
While dolphins poke their heads, eager to win.

The tide comes in, it takes a stroll,
Searching for treasures, the sand's a hole.
A flip-flop's fate is always quite grim,
But laughter's the tide that'll always swim.

So here's to the joys that the beach bestows,
With belly flops that make everyone doze.
Grab your sunscreen, but don't forget fun,
In this cozy chaos, there's always a pun.

## Salty Sighs at Dusk

As the sun sets, the shadows grow,
Petty fights with surfboards, oh what a show!
Fish tales taller than the waves we ride,
While crabs do the moonwalk and glide.

Pineapple hats and sunglasses on tight,
Beachgoers groaning about the bite.
Sand between toes, a mischievous bug,
Forgetting a towel, is that a good hug?

Shells whisper secrets, if only they could,
Of seaweed bungee jumping, oh how they would!
But hear the giggles as kids take a fall,
It's just part of life in this sandy ball.

With salty breezes and clouds in a swirl,
The sound of laughter makes the heart twirl.
So let's belly flop under the twilight gleam,
And let those salty sighs drift into a dream.

## Echoes of the Deep

In the morning light, fish do a jig,
While turtles sunbathe, all cozy and big.
Octopuses hide in their multi-armed flair,
While starfish giggle without a care.

A surfer's wipeout becomes the main show,
With beach balls bouncing, oh what a blow!
As seagulls squawk about stolen fries,
We learn that the ocean has no goodbyes.

Find a conch shell, hear the ocean's voice,
Whispering giggles, it's hard to rejoice.
A jellyfish floats by, like a jelly on toast,
We laugh and we cheer for this quirky host.

So dive right in, make a splash in good cheer,
For the echoes of the deep are all found here.
With every giggle and wave we adore,
Life in the surf is just never a bore.

## **Nightfall on Sandy Shores**

The sun dips low with a wink and a wave,
Wide-eyed children, like mermaids, they crave.
As fireworks fizzle like stars in a blast,
We dance on the sand, hoping this night lasts.

There's laughter in the breeze, so wild and free,
While jellyfish glow like tacos at sea.
A starfish on a skateboard, oh what a sight,
Cruising the coastline under moonlight.

Tide pools giggle with bubbles galore,
A crab plays tag, who could ask for more?
With marshmallows toasting over the fire's light,
We'll spin tales so silly, it stretches the night.

So let's sing with the waves, embrace the breeze,
As the stars drop in for a giggling tease.
In the nightfall's embrace, joy swells like a song,
Where laughter is endless, and we all belong.

## Lucid Waters

Bubbles pop like soda fizz,
Fish dance like they're on a quiz,
Seashells whisper silly jokes,
While crabs strut like fancy folks.

Jellyfish wobble, quite the show,
Waves curling, with laughter, go,
Starfish giggle, arms in a twist,
Under the waves, nothing's amiss.

Sandcastles lean, a fragile dream,
Seagulls plot with a cheeky scheme,
The tide pulls in, like a friend's embrace,
In this blue world, there's not a trace.

Splash fights brewing, with lots of cheer,
Floating toys and drinks so near,
Sunsets giggle as they retreat,
In lucid waters, life's a treat.

## The Sigh of Salt Air

Seagulls squawk with comic flair,
Whispers float in salty air,
Waves crash down like jesters tumble,
While fish recount their grandest fumble.

Driftwood tales of pirates bold,
Mermaids laugh, or so I'm told,
Sandpipers sprint in a silly race,
Crabs throwing shade, can't keep pace.

The tide rolls in, a ticklish friend,
With every splash, laughter won't end,
Coconut hats that float on by,
In this quirky sea, oh my!

Shells sing songs, both sweet and sly,
As dolphins leap to say goodbye,
The sun takes off with a funny glare,
Leaving behind the sigh of salt air.

## Peace in the Brackish Depths

Eels play peek-a-boo with glee,
Turtles wave as they glide free,
The brackish depths, a comic spot,
Where sea cucumbers dance a lot.

Crabs crack jokes with sideways flair,
While flounders flash a puzzled stare,
Octopus chefs flip a fishy dish,
In this deep realm, it's not amiss.

Rays glide by wearing snazzy shades,
As laughter echoes, fun cascades,
Sea slugs shuffle with awkward grace,
Creating smiles in every place.

At peace down here, where waves won't pout,
Life's a party, without a doubt,
And when fish giggle, so do we,
In the brackish depths, wild and free.

## Solace at Sea

Sailboats wobble, a merry sight,
With sails flapping, a comical flight,
The horizon giggles, waves applaud,
As scuba divers play the fraud.

Surfers hum a cheerful tune,
While dolphins dance beneath the moon,
Beach balls bounce with playful ease,
Saltwater tickles in the breeze.

Mermaids grin, painting the skies,
With rainbow hues and silly ties,
Coconuts roll, a jolly spree,
Finding solace, just you and me.

At twilight's call, the giggles soar,
In a world of waves, we'll always explore,
For every splash is a giggly key,
Unlocking joy and a spirit free.

## Rhythms of Rest by the Shore

Waves crash gently, a bubbly song,
Seagulls squawk loud, where they belong.
Footprints in sand, a clumsy parade,
Shells sing tunes, a serenade.

Children giggle, as buckets spill,
Sandcastles tumble with rising thrill.
A crab steals lunch, oh what a sight,
Making us laugh, in pure delight.

Sunsets splatter with colors bold,
Tails of dolphins in stories told.
Fish dive down, with a funny flip,
As laughter bubbles from every lip.

Breezes tease with a salty cheer,
Floaties drift by, with no hint of fear.
As night falls softly, stars poke shy,
Moon joins the dance, oh my, oh my!

## **Tidals of Tranquility**

Gentle waves whisper secrets old,
While crabs in tuxedos are brave and bold.
Starfish lounge, catching daytime rays,
While jellyfish glide in a shimmering haze.

Seashells wear hats, pretending to sleep,
As sea turtles dance, not a soul to keep.
Every splash carries giggles anew,
Sand dollars chuckle, with a playful crew.

The sun peeks through the fluffy white,
Tickling the waves, oh what a sight!
Fish flash smiles as they swim on by,
Creating ripples, oh me, oh my!

As evening nears, the crickets play,
With waves in sync, we laugh and sway.
In the playful tide, dreams take flight,
Joyful hearts sing beneath the night.

## Swaying with the Seaweed

Seaweed dances with a bouncy flair,
Wiggling and jigging without a care.
Fish join in, doing the twist,
In this aquatic party, none are missed.

Crabby grumbles, "Why not take a dip?"
While seagulls giggle and take a slip.
Mermaids laugh, tossing shells with glee,
As sea stars spin, feeling so free.

Tides pull and push like a playful friend,
Every wave's a joke, the laughs don't end.
Salt on our lips, the sun overhead,
With silly shenanigans, we dance instead.

For as the tide rolls, and the sun waves bye,
We'll find the humor, and sigh a happy sigh.
With dreams stuffed full of ocean's jest,
We lay down our heads, in perfect rest.

# Sweet Slumber on Salted Sands

Under the sun, we sprawl and sigh,
Waves play peek-a-boo as gulls fly by.
Naps interrupted by a playful splash,
Sand tickles toes in a cheery flash.

Flip-flops forgotten, a funky fashion,
Bikini tops turn into seashell passion.
With each soft wave, we drift away,
In this sandy dreamland, we wish to stay.

Seashells chatter, with secrets to share,
As giggles float up on the warm sea air.
The sunset grins, a big goofy guy,
Cramming the clouds full of blush and pie.

So snuggle close, with a sandy embrace,
Laughing aloud in this happy place.
Then close your eyes, let bliss take your hand,
For magic unfolds on this salted land.

**Whispered Tales from the Tide**

Tiny fish have silly dreams,
Dancing under moonlit beams.
Seagulls snicker as they dive,
Wishing they could learn to jive.

Crabs in suits, a wedding dance,
Pinching guests just for a chance.
Turtles sport their snazzy ties,
While dolphins wear their best disguise.

## **Crests of Calm**

Waves that giggle, splash and play,
Chasing shells that run away.
Octopus throws a fancy bash,
His party tricks are quite the splash!

Starfish sit in a gossip ring,
Sharing tales of the latest fling.
Seashells whisper secrets low,
As waves come in and say hello.

### The Nautical Nocturne


Mermaids come with hair so bright,
Singing songs throughout the night.
But fish who've heard it all before,
Just roll their eyes and swim for shore.

Dolphins laughing, flipping high,
Pretend they're clouds up in the sky.
While plankton shimmer, oh so neat,
Hosting raves beneath our feet.

**Breaths of the Briny Deep**

Barnacles hold a talent show,
With crabs who tap, it steals the show.
Jellyfish float without a care,
Lighting up like they're rare flair.

Anglerfish sport their glowing gear,
Casting lights, they bring good cheer.
In this realm where laughs don't cease,
Every wave brings joy and peace.

## Harmonies of the Horizon

Seashells dance and sing with glee,
Fish in tuxedos sipping tea.
Crabs in line for the conga line,
Salty disco, oh so fine!

Dolphins flip with grace and flair,
Seagulls gossip without a care.
The tide rolls in with a playful sigh,
Shells are laughing, oh my my!

## Waves of Serenity

Gentle waves toss about a tale,
Seasick seagulls who fail to sail.
Sandy feet with a wink and grin,
Mermaids giggle, come join in!

Naughty octopuses play hide and seek,
Tickling toes with their sly little sneak.
Crabs cracking jokes in the evening glow,
Who knew the shore could put on a show?

**The Sea's Gentle Embrace**

Under the sun, the sardines prance,
Starfish waltz in a watery dance.
Clams flip-flop in a lazy sway,
"Shell we dance?" they shout, hooray!

Turtles relaxing with snacks galore,
Slurping seaweed, then asking for more.
"Who ordered this party?" fish chuckle loud,
A splashy fiesta, it's quite a crowd!

## **Beneath Starlit Waters**

Ocean whispers tickle the night,
Glimmering fish in a fancy flight.
Eels wearing ties, looking quite sly,
Under the starlight, they flutter by!

Jellyfish float with a gentle sway,
Glow-in-the-dark in a charming display.
"Swim this way!" calls a cheeky crab,
Join the party, no need to grab!

## Sheltered by the Sea

A crab in a tux, quite dapper and neat,
He dances on sand, with two left feet.
Seagulls squawk tunes, they croon from the sky,
Fish all take bets, on who'll win the pie.

A starfish held court, with a sassy old shell,
Claiming his throne, where the barnacles dwell.
The jellyfish giggle, in their wobbly glee,
While sunburnt tourists spill drinks on the spree.

The tide rolls in, with a cheeky wave's wink,
Saying, 'Hey humans, what's your plans for a drink?'
With beach balls a-bouncing, the laughter rounds,
As seashells all witness the fun that abounds.

So come take a swim, in this playful blue,
Where silliness reigns, with a splash or two.
In this little cove, where the wild things roam,
The sea's friendly whispers feel just like home.

## Resonance in the Foam

Bubbles and giggles, a frothy delight,
Squids wearing glasses say 'Isn't this rite?'
The octopus juggles, with ink in his style,
All of us here are just here for a smile.

Crabs playing tag on a sandy soft track,
While dolphins dive under, then leap, then come back.
A pirate parrot squawks tales from the sky,
Claiming riches from treasure, but just eats pie.

The waves hum a tune, a funny old song,
Where surfboards dance, as they glide all night long.
The tides play the rhythm, of laughter and cheer,
In this bubbly ballet, let go of your fear.

So come join the fun, let the foam be your guide,
With silliness swirling, there's no need to hide.
In this water ballet, let your worries roam free,
For here in the laughter, we're all just like tea.

## Oceanscape of Night

Stars hang like jellybeans, twinkling so bright,
While fish in pajamas swim past with delight.
The moon's wearing shades, with an oceanfront view,
As crabs launch a dance party, just for the crew.

A walrus in glasses, reading the tide,
Says 'Let's mix it up, oh, come take a ride!'
With seaweed confetti, the night comes alive,
As dolphins serenade, they twist and they dive.

The waves clap their hands, with a splish and a splash,
As party hats float by, in a colorful dash.
The night tides are laughing, with dreams that don't stop,
In the oceanscape's bliss, we all hop and bop.

So laugh with the tides, let your worries all float,
As sea creatures dance, and the night keeps you afloat.
In this whimsical dream, set your troubles apart,
For the oceanscape's joy is a song for the heart.

## Deep Sea Reflections

In the murky deep, where the fish make a fuss,
The anglerfish frowns, says, 'What's all the fuss?'
With a light on his head, and a grin that's so sly,
He'll lure in a dance, and then teach you to fly.

A turtle in sneakers, moving right slow,
Claims he knows secrets no one else knows.
While pufferfish puff, in a comical feat,
They giggle with glee at the rhythm of beat.

The squids perform puzzles, in colors so bright,
Drawing maps of the sparkle, in the deep, starry night.
While sea cucumbers giggle, submerged in their glee,
Saying, 'Hey, isn't life just a tasty sea spree?'

So dive in the depths, let the laughter unfold,
Where the fish play the notes that the ocean has told.
In these deep sea reflections, let joy be the theme,
For laughter is the tide that will wash you downstream.

## Lullabies of the Blue

Under waves where fish can dance,
Sea turtles spin in a funny prance.
The crabs do cartwheels, oh what a sight,
As starfish giggle, glowing at night.

A dolphin sings in a silly tone,
Teasing the seals all cuddled in foam.
The jellyfish wave their tentacled hands,
While schools of fish form musical bands.

Seagulls squawk jokes from high above,
They're the comedians, full of love.
In the depths where laughter floats,
Sardines gather for punchline quotes.

So close your eyes and drift away,
With dreams of fish who love to play.
In this world of giggles, bright and true,
Sleep tight as the ocean sings for you.

## **Resting by the Reef**

Coral beds where clownfish smile,
They tickle sea urchins for a while.
The parrotfish giggle, munching their snack,
While the pufferfish puffs, keeping it whack.

Crabs take naps, snoring in style,
Their backward walks always make us smile.
Anemones sway, playing peekaboo,
As octopuses tell tales, all brand new.

The sun sets low, casting a gleam,
Fish gather 'round to share a dream.
Jellybeans float in this underwater spree,
Where everyone knows it's fun to be free.

With laughter echoing off the sand,
Nature's humor, simply grand.
So rest your head, let worries cease,
In this funny reef, find your peace.

## The Calm Between Storms

Waves gently rock as seagulls squawk,
While crabs play cards on the sandy dock.
A walrus tells jokes, in his furry coat,
Making fish giggle as they float.

The lighthouse winks with its guiding light,
As playful waves leap with delight.
An otter slides down with grace and fun,
While the breeze tickles everyone.

Stars above share secrets all night,
As laughter echoes in pure delight.
Fish form a choir in perfect tune,
Singing sweet songs under the moon.

So take a breath, let worries part,
With ocean humor close to heart.
In the calm where silliness thrives,
Joyful moments feel so alive.

## Nautical Nightfall

As sun dips down, the waves come alive,
Seashells chuckle as crabs arrive.
Starfish perform in the fading light,
With sea cucumbers, the comical sight.

Mollusks giggle, sticking out tongues,
Making faces, oh, how they've sung!
The moon peeks down, playing hide and seek,
While squids squirt ink with a playful tweak.

Mermaids share stories, all wrapped in jest,
Telling of fish with glittery vests.
A chorus of bubbles rises above,
In the salty breeze, we find our love.

So let the starlit waters embrace,
With humor and joy in this blissful space.
As the night unfolds, drift and sway,
To the funny rhythms of a watery ballet.

## Lull in the Surf

Waves rolling in with a giggly cheer,
Seagulls squawking, they're loud but near.
Fish in the sea do their silly dance,
Shells whisper secrets of an underwater romance.

Sandcastles topple, oh what a sight,
Crabs hold a party, they dance with delight.
Tides tickle toes, with a gentle embrace,
While dolphins jump high, it's a splashy race.

Laughter echoes through salty air,
As octopuses juggle, a sight so rare.
Starfish play tag on the ocean floor,
While a clam hums tunes, who could ask for more?

So close your eyes, let the sea be your friend,
With each wave's whisper, let your worries end.
Drift off on dreams, with a giggle and grin,
In the lull of the surf, let the fun begin!

## Melodies of the Blue

Bubbles pop like a fizzy drink,
As fish flirt around, they slyly wink.
Turtles play poker, oh what a game,
While seaweed dances, it's never the same.

Jellyfish sway, with a glow in the night,
Squids ink stories in fancy flight.
A whale sings out, but off-key it goes,
While mermaid auditions are full of nose blows.

Salty mist tickles a sleepy seal,
Who dreams of sardines with an exciting appeal.
Crashing waves hum a tune like a harp,
As sea urchins laugh, "Hey, it's time to get sharp!"

Close those curtains of eyelids so tight,
Let the funny sea tales bring you delight.
In a world full of giggles beneath the bright moon,
You'll find joy in their melodies, sleepy soft tune.

## Beneath the Starry Sea

Under the waves where the sea stars glow,
A crab tells jokes, quite the funny show.
Goby fish giggle, they play hide and seek,
While a plankton band plays tunes of the week.

Octopus chefs whip up meals with flair,
While shrimp put on wigs, it's a wacky affair.
Coral reefs sparkle, a colorful mess,
As clownfish make faces, they want to impress.

Lobsters recite poetry, with pinchers so grand,
Each rhyme is a treasure, sea-inspired and planned.
The murmurs of waves sing a lullaby soft,
With laughter and giggles that carry aloft.

So float on your dreams in this whimsical sea,
Where each little creature is zany and free.
With stars shining bright, they cradle your sleep,
In the funny tide's arms, let your worries leap!

## Serene Shores of Sleep

Morning unfolds with a splash and a smile,
As sea foam tickles, it floats for a while.
Seagulls parade with their silly squawks,
Stealing your sandwich while you enjoy walks.

The sun plays hide and seek with the tide,
While dolphins surf in, ready to ride.
A walrus wears sunglasses, quite the sight,
Sipping on seaweed, getting cozy tonight.

With starfish in slippers, they dance on the shore,
Finding lost treasures, and giggling galore.
Clams clap their shells, setting a beat,
As waves join the chorus, so lively and sweet.

So snuggle your blanket, let the dream waves sweep,
To the shores of slumber, where silliness leaps.
Feel the gentle nudge, as you softly sway,
In this serene world where laughter will play!

**Soothing Surf Serenades**

Waves giggle as they rush to the sand,
Tickling feet, so soft and grand.
Seagulls squawk a silly tune,
Dancing crabs beneath the moon.

Shells play maracas, swaying right,
The ocean's jests, a real delight.
Fish in tuxedos swim with cheer,
Making sure the fun's sincere!

Surfboards wobble, riders fall,
Splashing water, laughter's call.
Where the salty breeze does tease,
And all worries drift with ease.

So come and join the sandy spree,
Where every wave is wild and free.
Bubbles rise, and giggles soar,
In the silly waves, who could ask for more?

## Moonlit Waters and Gentle Rhythms

Under the moon, the waters wink,
Mermaids giggle as they sip their drink.
Starfish spin in a dance so bright,
Crabs wear shades, oh what a sight!

Ripples whisper jokes to shells,
Conch shells echoed, ringing bells.
Jellyfish jiggle, floating high,
While sea turtles wave goodbye.

Seashells tell tales of love so grand,
Innocent romances on the sand.
With tides that tickle and tease the shore,
Even the seaweed begs for more!

As the surf serenades all night,
A funny kingdom in soft twilight.
Dreams are woven with salty threads,
Understated charm, where laughter spreads.

## Tranquil Tides, Silent Songs

Whispers of water and silly sighs,
Fish with glasses, oh, how they rise!
Seashells laugh in the gentle breeze,
    Chasing after playful tease.

Beach balls bounce like a happy pup,
    Finding fish who don't give up.
The horizon giggles, stretching wide,
As seagulls spin with pompous pride.

Bubble parties beneath the sun,
Where starfish and seaweed have their fun.
Even the waves can't help but grin,
In this splashy world, let the jokes begin!

Softly the night wraps around the sea,
And laughter drifts like wild set free.
With every wave, a chuckle's drift,
    A melody of joy, the ocean's gift!

## **Silent Songs**

Waves roll in with a clumsy gait,
Fishy friends throw a quirky fate.
Starfish wear hats, oh what a show,
Splashing humor everywhere they go!

Silent songs from beneath the tide,
With grinning dolphins as their guide.
Coral reefs burst with laughter bright,
All basking in the glowing light.

Twinkling tides that tickle your toes,
Whimsical whispers where happiness flows.
Every foam bubble a cheerful cheer,
In the underwater realm of fun so dear.

So take a seat on the sandy floor,
As the sea sends giggles to our shore.
In playful jests, the sea takes flight,
A comic wonder, pure delight!

**Cradle of the Coral**

In the cradle where bright colors spin,
Clownfish prepare for the silly win.
Corals hum with laughter bare,
As sea urchins pull a funny hair!

Sandy shores hide goofy things,
Where the ocean's laughter sings.
Nudibranchs, dressed in quirky wear,
Join in jests without a care.

The tides come in with a playful roll,
Tickling toes, making hearts whole.
Crabs wearing hats strut with pride,
In this whimsical world, join the ride!

As day turns to light, and night to dreams,
Laughter reflects in the moonlit beams.
In this cradle, all fears subside,
For joy is riding the ocean's tide.

www.ingramcontent.com/pod-product-compliance
Lightning Source LLC
Chambersburg PA
CBHW060145230426
43661CB00003B/571